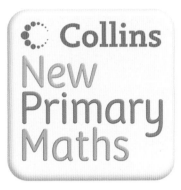

Pupil Book 3A

Series Editor: Peter Clarke

Authors: Jeanette Mumford, Sandra Roberts, Andrew Edmondson

Contents

Mobile numbers

● **Read and write numbers to at least 1000 and put them in order**

 ① Write the numbers on each mobile in words.

a

26
59   44

b
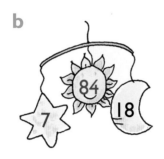
84
7   18

c
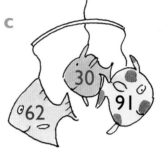
30
62   91

d
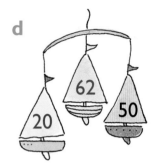
62
20   50

② How many tens are in each **red** number?

③ How many units are in each **blue** number?

④ Write these numbers using figures.

a eight   b zero   c twenty-five   d seventy-four   e twelve

> **Example**
>
> 36 has 3 tens

 ① Write the numbers on each mobile in words.

a

492   382   517

b
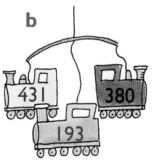
431   380
193

c

903   201
300

d

996
267   75

② How many tens are in each **red** number?

③ How many units are in each **blue** number?

④ How many hundreds are in each **black** number?

The last 3 digits of Toni's mobile phone number are 4, 6 and 9.

a Find all the possible numbers she could have.

b Order the numbers from smallest to largest.

Fruit card ordering

● **Read and write ordinal numbers to at least 100**

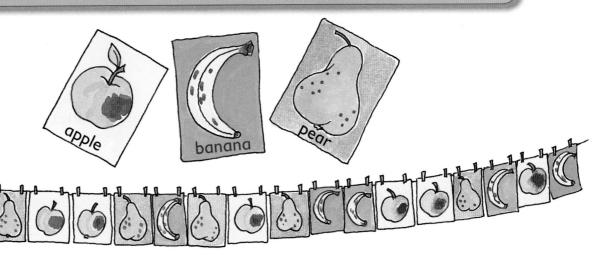

 ① Write down the name of the fruit in these positions.

a 3rd	b 1st	c ninth	d 7th
e tenth	f 13th	g twentieth	h 18th

② Write the positions of all the pears.

 Work in pairs.

A B C D E F G H I J K L M N O P Q R S T U V W X Y Z
1st 3rd   20th

Write down a three-letter or four-letter word without letting your partner see. Then write down the position of each letter.

Show each other your position numbers and find your partner's word.

Write three more words each.

Your word is CAT.

 Follow the instruction.

4th, 18th, 1st, 23rd	1st	2nd, 9th, 7th

8th, 1st, 16th, 16th, 25th	6th, 1st, 3rd, 5th

Find the groups

● **Count the collections by grouping**

Hit the target
Play in pairs.

How to play:

● Choose a number card. This is your target number.
● Take turns to roll the dice.
● Look at the number on the dice and take the number of ones cube(s).
● Keep taking turns to roll the dice and collect the matching number of ones cubes.
● When you can make a ten, swap the ten ones cubes for a tens rod.
● The first player to reach the target number wins.
● Choose another number card and repeat.

Each pair needs:

● 5 number cards from 50 to 99
● 1–6 dice
● base 10 materials (tens and ones)

 For each picture work out:

● how many groups   ● how many in each group   ● how many altogether

Example

> 4 groups
> 5 in each group
> 4 × 5 = 20

a   b

c   d

   e

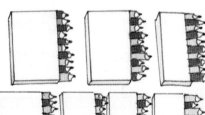

 For each picture in the question above, double the amount then double it again.

Example

a   20 → 40 → 80

Counting blocks

● Count on in steps of 3, 4 or 5 from any number and back

Add or subtract the number shown on the blocks to complete the number sequences.

a 2, 6, ——, ——, 18, ——, ——, 30

b 3, 8, 13, ——, ——, ——, ——, ——

c 1, 4, ——, ——, ——, ——, 19, ——

d 50, 45, 40, ——, ——, ——, ——, ——

e 40, 36, ——, ——, ——, ——, ——, ——

1 Number cards up to 40 that are multiples of 3 and multiples of 4 have been sorted.
Three cards are missing. What are the missing numbers and where do they belong?

2 Draw your own sorting diagrams like the ones below.

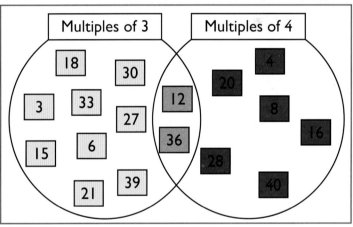

Sort the numbers 1–40 to match the labels. Write any numbers that belong in both sets in the middle.

a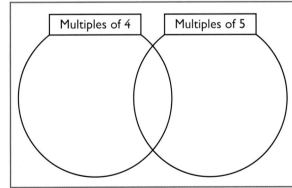
Multiples of 4   Multiples of 5

b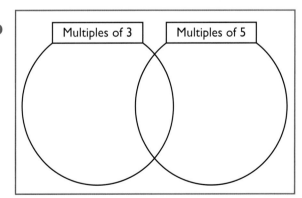
Multiples of 3   Multiples of 5

Look at your sorting diagrams for question **2** above.

a List the multiples of 6.   **b** List the multiples of 10.

Winning numbers

 Split a number into hundreds, tens and ones

1 Write each of the following numbers using expanded notation.

a 268   b 314   c 957

d 475   e 680   f 501

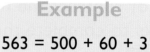

Example

563 = 500 + 60 + 3

2 Write the total number.

a 300 + 60 + 7   b 800 + 20 + 5

c 100 + 70 + 9   d 400 + 0 + 6

e 900 + 10 + 0   f 700 + 50 + 5

 Copy and complete by writing > or < between each pair of numbers.

a 145 ☐ 99   b 425 ☐ 524   c 369 ☐ 396

d 706 ☐ 670   e 819 ☐ 869   f 541 ☐ 512

 a Use 2 or 3 place value cards each time.
Make as many different 3-digit numbers as you can.

b Now order your numbers, smallest to largest.

You need:
- 6 place value cards

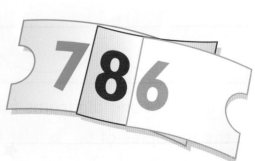

Addition facts book

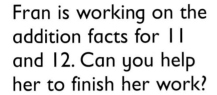

● **Know addition facts for each number to 20**

Fran is working on the addition facts for 11 and 12. Can you help her to finish her work?

11	12
$11 + 0 = 11$	$12 + 0 = 12$
$10 + \square = 11$	$\square + 11 = 12$
$9 + \square = 11$	$2 + \square = 12$
$\square + 3 = 11$	$\square + 9 = 12$
$7 + \square = 11$	$4 + \square = 12$
$\square + 5 = \square$	$5 + \square = 12$
	$\square + \square = 12$

Jill has written the addition facts for the number 14.

Following the same pattern, write down the addition facts for the numbers that Max, Nisha and Leah have chosen.

14

14

$14 + 0 = 14$
$13 + 1 = 14$
$12 + 2 = 14$
$11 + 3 = 14$
$10 + 4 = 14$
$9 + 5 = 14$
$8 + 6 = 14$
$7 + 7 = 14$

a  17

b  20

c 19

❶ Millie is using her addition facts to work out multiples of 10 that equal 180. Can you finish her work?

❷ Use your addition facts to write out the multiples of 10 that equal 100.

$180 + 0 = 180$
$170 + 10 = 180$

Fish food numbers

● **Know subtraction facts for each number to 20**

Each fish can eat two pieces of food at a time. Find pairs of numbers on the food where the difference equals the number on the fish.

Example

16 − 5 = 11

Work out four meals for each fish.

1 Work out five meals for each fish.

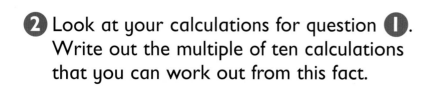

2 Look at your calculations for question **1**. Write out the multiple of ten calculations that you can work out from this fact.

I know 18 − 2 is 16 so I can work out 180 − 20 is 160.

Explain why these calculations go together.

13 − 5 = 8   130 − 50 = 80

Balloon tens

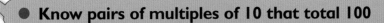
● **Know pairs of multiples of 10 that total 100**

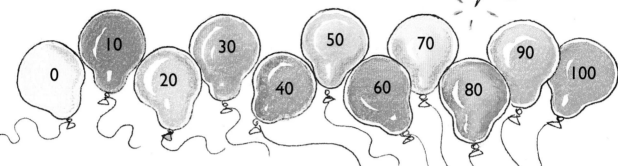

1 Write out the multiples of 10 from 10 to 100.

10, 20, … 100.

2 Write the next multiple of 10.

a 60	b 30	c 50	d 10
e 90	f 0	g 20	h 70

3 Write the previous multiple of 10.

a 70	b 90	c 40	d 20
e 100	f 30	g 80	h 60

1 Write out the calculation, filling in the missing multiple of 10.

a ☐ + 80 = 100   f ☐ + 100 = 100

b 60 + ☐ = 100   g ☐ + 40 = 100

c 90 + ☐ = 100   h 10 + ☐ = 100

d 50 + ☐ = 100   i 20 + ☐ = 100

e 70 + ☐ = 100   j ☐ + 30 = 100

2 Now look at the calculations again and write the number fact for 10 that helps you remember it.

What are the pairs of multiples of 5 that total 100? Here is one: 35 + 65

Fairground addition

● **Add mentally combinations of one-digit and two-digit numbers**

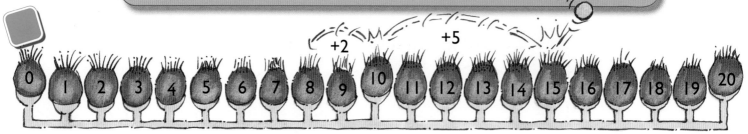

+2   +5

1 Use the number line to help you jump to the next number.

a Start at 8, add on 7 = ☐   b Start at 9, add on 6 = ☐
c Start at 7, add on 5 = ☐   d Start at 9, add on 8 = ☐
e Start at 5, add on 9 = ☐   f Start at 6, add on 7 = ☐

2 Now work out where to start on the number line and finish these calculations.

a 25 + 8 = ☐   c 23 + 9 = ☐   e 29 + 3 = ☐
b 27 + 5 = ☐   d 26 + 7 = ☐   f 29 + 9 = ☐

Choose a number on a frog and a duck to make an addition calculation in your head. Write down *how* you did the calculation. Your teacher will tell you how many calculations to make.

Choose five of your calculations from the  section above.

Write a sentence about each, using the vocabulary in the box.

Example

56 + 9 = 65
The sum of 56 and 9 is 65.

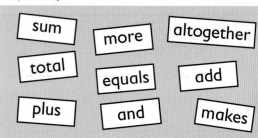

sum   more   altogether
total   equals   add
plus   and   makes

Subtraction juggling

Subtract mentally combinations of one-digit and two-digit numbers

 Work out the subtraction calculations, using the jugglers' balls number line to help you.

(1) (2) (3) (4) (5) (6) (7) (8) (9) (10) (11) (12) (13) (14) (15) (16) (17) (18) (19) (20)

a (15) – (4) = ☐   f (19) – (6) = ☐

b (14) – (5) = ☐   g (18) – (7) = ☐

c (11) – (3) = ☐   h (12) – (6) = ☐

d (17) – (8) = ☐   i (20) – (9) = ☐

e (13) – (7) = ☐   j (16) – (5) = ☐

 Choose two numbers, one from each of the jugglers' balls. Use the two numbers to make a subtraction calculation. Work out the answer in your head and then write down how you did it. Your teacher will tell you how many calculations to make.

53 73 11 31 42 24

9 8 4 5 7 6

 Choose five of your calculations from the 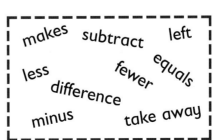 section above. Write a sentence about each, using the vocabulary in the box.

makes subtract left
less equals
fewer
difference
minus take away

Example

31 – 6 = 25
The difference between 31 and 6 is 25.

Number line race game

● Know addition and subtraction facts for each number to 20

Race to 6
A game for 2 players.
How to play:
● Decide who will be moving from 1 to 6 and from 12 to 6.
● Place your counter on 1 or 12.
● Take turns to roll the dice and add or subtract the dice number to or from your counter number.
● Before moving your counter, say the related calculation.
● The winner is the first person to reach 6.
● Now swap directions and play again.

You need:
● 2 counters in different colours
● 1-6 dice

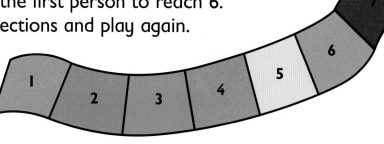

Race to 10
A game for 2 players.
How to play:
● Decide who will be moving from 1 to 10 and from 20 to 10.
● Place your counter on 1 or 20.
● Take turns to roll the dice and add or subtract the dice number to or from your counter number.
● Before moving your counter, say the related calculation.
● The winner is the first person to reach 10.
● Now swap directions and play again.

You need:
● 2 counters in different colours
● 0–9 dice

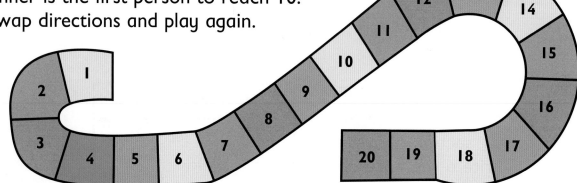

Use the ● board to play the game you played as a class at the start of the lesson. Each player rolls the dice 10 times. Who is closer to 10?

Summer fruits

● Know sums and differences of multiples of 10

 Use these multiples of ten to make addition and subtraction calculations. Your teacher will tell you how many addition and how many subtraction calculations to make.

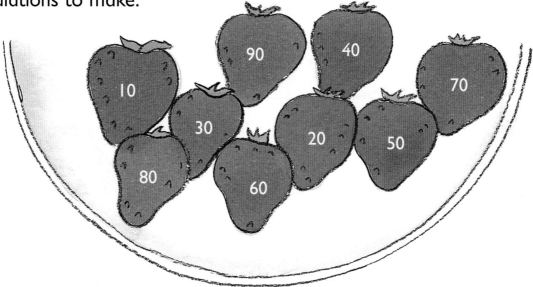

Choose a number from the bowl. Write down a pair of multiples of 10 whose sum equals this number and a pair with a difference of this number. Your teacher will tell you how many addition and how many subtraction calculations to make.

 Choose a number from the cherry bowl in the ● activity. Write down all the possible pairs of multiples of 10 with this total.

Thinking about shopping

● **Solve one-step and two-step word problems**

Solve the children's shopping problems. Show all your working out.

a It costs 45p for one ticket into the fair. How much does it cost for two tickets?

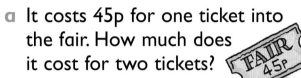

b I have 50p, 10p and 20p in my hand. I see 10p on the ground. How much will I have if I pick it up?

c Every week I save 20p. I have been saving for 7 weeks. How much do I have?

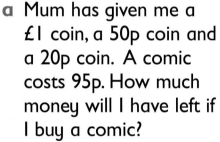

d Crisps are 25p a packet. I bought 3 packets. **i** How much money did I spend?

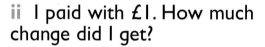

ii I paid with £1. How much change did I get?

a Mum has given me a £1 coin, a 50p coin and a 20p coin. A comic costs 95p. How much money will I have left if I buy a comic?

b I save 30p a week. I have been saving for 5 weeks. How many more weeks will I need to save to buy a book for £1.80?

c Dad gave me £5 to share between me and my three sisters. How much do we have each?

d I have bought a notepad that cost 85p. I paid the exact amount with four coins. What were they?

Make up a two-step word problem to go with £10 − £3.40 − £1.65. What is the answer?

Jars of odds and evens

● **Describe and extend number sequences of odd and even numbers to at least 100**

Complete the number sequences on the jam jars, then say whether the numbers are odd or even.

Example

2 4 6 8 10 → _even_

even!

0 2 4 6 8

a 1 3 5 ___ 9 → _____

b 13 15 ___ 19 21 → _____

odd!

c 8 10 12 14 ___ → _____

d 20 22 24 ___ ___ → _____

1 3 5 7 9

e 17 ___ 21 23 25 → _____

f 27 29 31 ___ ___ → _____

❶ Sort the numbers on the pickles into odd and even.
For each jar, write down all of the odd numbers and all of the even numbers.

a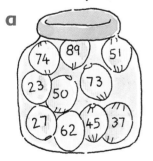

b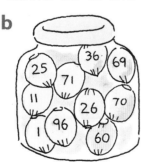

c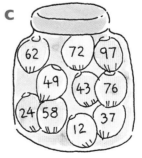

d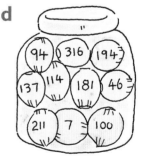

❷ Draw your own pickle jar containing ten numbers. Ask a friend to sort them into odd and even.

Use the digit cards 2, 4 and 7.
a Make 6 different 3-digit numbers.
b Sort them into odd or even.
c Choose 3 different cards which will make more odd than even numbers.

You need:
● 0–9 digit cards

Fishy odds and evens

 ● **Find numbers that match a property**

1 Add together the even numbers on each boat.
Is the answer odd or even?

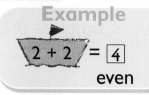

Example
2 + 2 = ☐4
even

a 4 + 4 = ☐   b 8 + 4 = ☐   c 10 + 4 = ☐

d 6 + 6 = ☐   e 8 + 6 = ☐   f 10 + 8 = ☐

2 Add together the odd numbers on each fish. Is the answer odd or even?

a 7 + 7 = ☐   b 3 + 5 = ☐   c 11 + 7 = ☐

d 9 + 9 = ☐   e 7 + 9 = ☐   f 13 + 3 = ☐

Test the rules
even + even = even
odd + odd = even

Test the rules
even + even = even
odd + odd = even

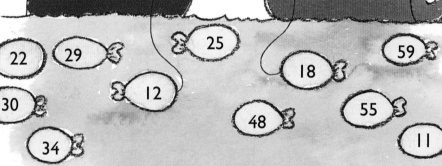

22   29   25   59
      12   18   43
30   55
      48   11
34

a Choose two fish with even numbers.
Write the sum and whether the answer is odd or even.
Do this for **8** pairs of even-numbered fish.

b Repeat for **8** pairs of odd-numbered fish.

Example

30 + 34 = 64
even

Test what happens when you add together an odd number and an even number.
Do this for **8** pairs of fish.
Write what you find as a rule.

Counting on and back

● Count on and back in steps of 2, 5 and 10

Add or subtract 2, 5 or 10 to complete each number sequence.

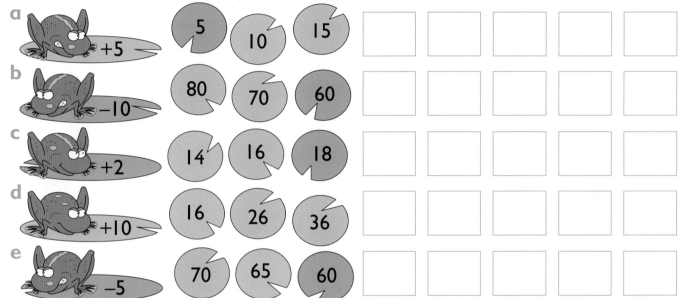

a +5 5 10 15

b −10 80 70 60

c +2 14 16 18

d +10 16 26 36

e −5 70 65 60

Copy and complete each number sequence.

a 7, 9, 11, 13, ☐, ☐, ☐, ☐, ☐

b 82, 72, 62, 52, ☐, ☐, ☐, ☐, ☐

c 13, 18, 23, 28, ☐, ☐, ☐, ☐, ☐

d 88, 86, 84, 82, ☐, ☐, ☐, ☐, ☐

e 1, 11, 21, 31, ☐, ☐, ☐, ☐, ☐

f 25, 27, 29, 31, ☐, ☐, ☐, ☐, ☐

g 99, 89, 79, 69, ☐, ☐, ☐, ☐, ☐

h 57, 52, 47, 42, ☐, ☐, ☐, ☐, ☐

i 13, 23, 33, 43, ☐, ☐, ☐, ☐, ☐

j 74, 69, 64, 59, ☐, ☐, ☐, ☐, ☐

● Choose one of the numbers.
● Secretly choose one of the patterns.
● Write a sequence of four numbers that contains your chosen number and uses the pattern you chose.
● Repeat this three more times.
● When you have finished, swap your four sequences with your partner.
● Write the next five numbers in each of your partner's four sequences.
● Then swap back and check each other's work.

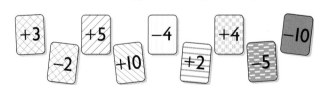

4 7 12 25 40 62 85 94 100

+3 −2 +5 +10 −4 +4 +2 −5 −10

19

Terrific tables

● **Know multiplication facts for the 2, 5 and 10 times tables**

Help the frogs to reach the other side by completing the number sequences on the lily pads.

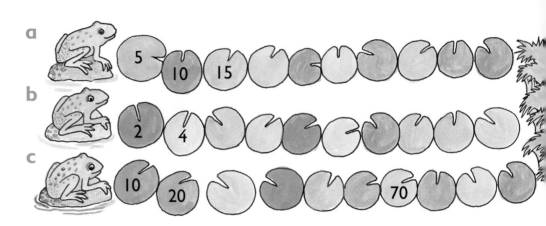

a
b
c

Knowing these key facts will help you learn the other number facts for the 2 times table.

1 × 2 = 2
2 × 2 = 4
5 × 2 = 10
10 × 2 = 20

Learn these key facts for the 5 times table. They will help you to work out the rest of the 5 times table.

1 × 5 = 5
2 × 5 = 10
5 × 5 = 25
10 × 5 = 50

Think of groups of 10 to help you with the 10 times table.

① Use the key facts for the 2 times table to help you answer these:

a
2 × 2 = ☐
3 × 2 = ☐
10 × 2 = ☐
9 × 2 = ☐

b
1 × 2 = ☐
4 × 2 = ☐
8 × 2 = ☐
7 × 2 = ☐

c
5 × 2 = ☐
6 × 2 = ☐
11 × 2 = ☐
0 × 2 = ☐

② Use the key facts for the 5 times table to help you answer these:

a
10 × 5 = ☐
9 × 5 = ☐
2 × 5 = ☐
3 × 5 = ☐

b
5 × 5 = ☐
4 × 5 = ☐
6 × 5 = ☐
7 × 5 = ☐

c
1 × 5 = ☐
8 × 5 = ☐
0 × 5 = ☐
11 × 5 = ☐

③ Now try the 10 times table.

a
2 × 10 = ☐
5 × 10 = ☐
1 × 10 = ☐

b
4 × 10 = ☐
6 × 10 = ☐
10 × 10 = ☐

c
7 × 10 = ☐
3 × 10 = ☐
8 × 10 = ☐

Write down the numbers 11 to 19. Multiply each of these by 2, 5 and 10. Which are easy? Which are more difficult? Why?

Fruit bowl division

● **Know division facts for the 2, 5 and 10 times tables**

Multiply the numbers on each piece of fruit by the number on the bowl.

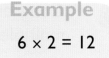

a

b

c

Write two multiplication and two division facts for each set of fruit.

Example

🍎 🍎 $4 \times 2 = 8$
🍎 🍎 $2 \times 4 = 8$
🍎 🍎 $8 \div 2 = 4$
🍎 🍎 $8 \div 4 = 2$

a

b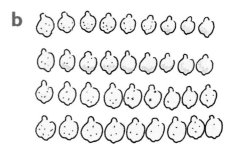

c

d

e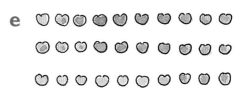

Write two multiplication facts and two division facts for each set of cards.

a   6   2   12

b   8   10   80

c   7   5   35

d   9   5   45

Multiples of 2, 5 and 10

● **Recognise two-digit and three-digit multiples of 2, 5 or 10**

Copy and complete the number sequences for the multiples of 2, 5 or 10.

a 52, 54, 56, □, □, □, □, □, □, □

b 102, 104, 106, 108, □, □, □, □, □, □

c 30, 40, 50, □, □, □, □, □, □, □

d 60, 65, 70, □, □, □, □, □, , □

e 105, 110, 115, □, □, □, □, □, □

f 100, 110, 120, □, □, □, □, □, □,

Each bag of marbles has one or two marbles that don't belong. Write which multiples are in the bag. Write down the one or two that don't belong.

Example

Multiples of 2: 200, 252, 268, 234, 286

241 is the odd one out.

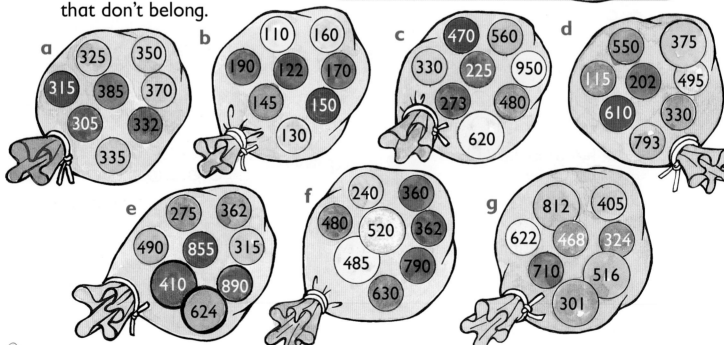

● Draw a bag of up to 10 marbles.
● Number the marbles.
● Ask your partner to find out which multiples are in the bag and which marbles don't belong.

Flower stall problems

● Solve word problems involving numbers in 'real life' and money

 Match the multiplication fact with its division fact.

| 3 × 4 = 12 | 8 × 10 = 80 | 6 × 5 = 30 | 7 × 2 = 14 | 5 × 3 = 15 | 10 × 4 = 40 |

| 80 ÷ 10 = 8 | 14 ÷ 2 = 7 | 40 ÷ 4 = 10 | 15 ÷ 3 = 5 | 12 ÷ 4 = 3 | 30 ÷ 5 = 6 |

Work out the answer to each of these word problems. Show all your working.

a Ricky buys 25 roses. He gives the same number of roses to his five friends. How many roses do they each get?

b Fran has a £20 note. She buys 3 lilies and receives £8 back in change. How much does each lily cost?

c The headteacher buys 80 sunflowers. She gives 10 to each class. How many classes are there?

d Ruksana buys 21 tulips and 14 roses. She puts 7 flowers in each vase. How many vases does she need?

e Buttercups come in bunches of 5 and cost £2 a bunch. Mr. Ahmed buys a total of 35 buttercups.
i How many bunches did he buy?
ii How much did this cost him?

f Daisies cost £20 for 10.
i How much does one daisy cost?
ii What is the cost of 12 daisies?

 Choose one multiplication fact and one division fact from the ▢ section and write a word problem about the flower stall for each fact.

Supermarket shapes

● **Recognise 3-D shapes from drawings**

Solids

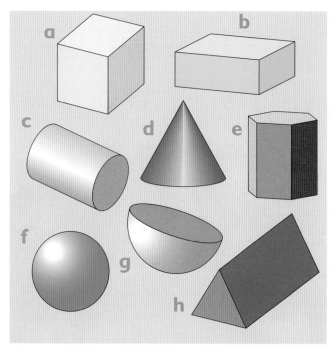

Shopping items

Match each solid to its picture.

Copy and complete this table.

Solid	Shopping item
a	5
b	
c	
d	

The box of tissues is a cube so goes with **a**.

Write the name of each solid in the correct column.

a Solid shapes

Solid	Prism	Not a prism
a	cube	
b		
c		

b Shopping items

Item	Prism	Not a prism
1		tin of soup
2		
3		

 Explain why a cylinder is not a prism.

Naming shapes

● **Recognise 2-D shapes from drawings**

For each shape, write its name and the number of sides.

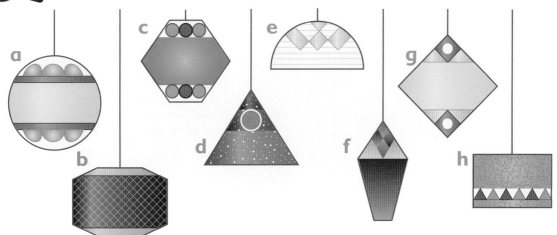

Example

triangle
3 sides

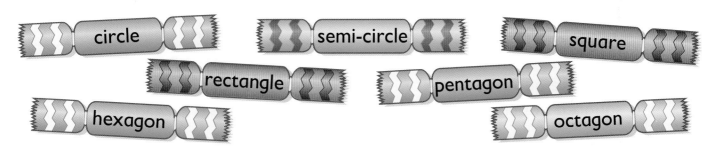

circle   semi-circle   square

rectangle   pentagon

hexagon   octagon

On I cm squared paper draw:

a 3 different pentagons

b 3 different hexagons

c 3 different octagons

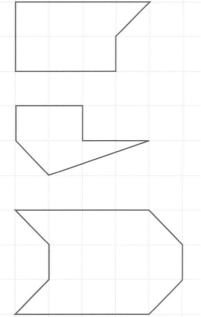

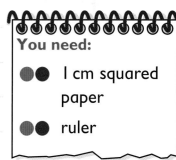

You need:

●● I cm squared paper

●● ruler

Draw two more different octagons.

Pick and choose shapes

● **Name and describe shapes**

Copy and complete the tables for this set of shapes.

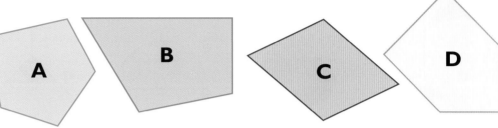

Shape	Four-sided	Sides same length
B	✔	✘
	✘	✘
	✔	✘
	✘	✘

Shape	Five vertices	1 or more right angles
	✔	✔
	✔	✔
	✘	✔
	✘	✘

Copy these quadrilaterals on to squared paper.

Mark the equal sides in blue.

Circle the right angles in red.

You need:
- ●●● set-square
- ●●● ruler
- ●● 1 cm squared paper
- ●● blue and red pencils

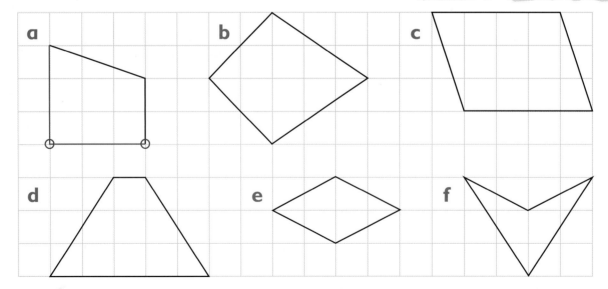

On your squared paper draw 6 different quadrilaterals.

Square dance

● **Recognise shapes from drawings**

You need:
● pinboard
● rubber band

1 Make these shapes on a pinboard.

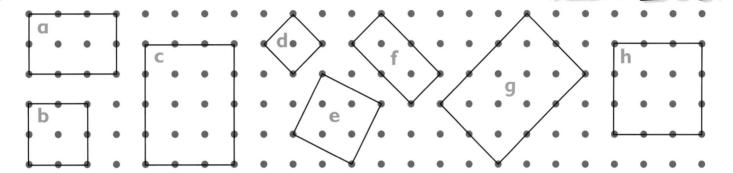

2 Copy and complete.

Shapes <u>b</u> are squares because each shape has ⎯ equal sides and ⎯ right-angled corners.

a Draw around the edges of the square card.

b Cut away a piece like this from the card.

c Place the card in its outline on the sheet of paper. Draw around the cut out to make this shape.

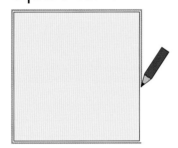

d Turn the card a $\frac{1}{4}$ turn. Draw around the cut out.

e Repeat step **d** two more times.

f Now colour your pattern.

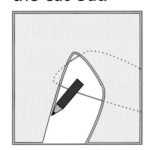

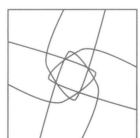

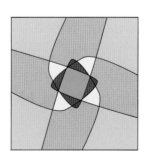

You need:
●● 8 cm square card
●● sheet of A4 paper
●● scissors
●● coloured pencils

What if your template is a regular pentagon?

Rocket patterns

• **Solve puzzles about shapes**

You need:

• 3 rectangles:
I red, I blue
and I yellow

 Fit your rectangles into the rocket outline to make different patterns. Here is one way.

Can you find five more?

Fit your rectangles into the rocket outline, using one of the following patterns.

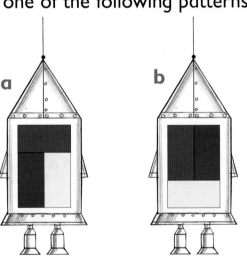

a   **b**

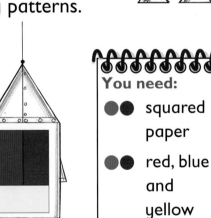

You need:

●● squared paper

●● red, blue and yellow pencils

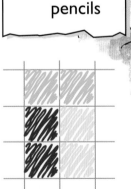

How many different ways can you fit your three rectangles into the rocket outline? Think of a way to record your answers. Here is an example.

 What if you had 4 rectangles? I red, I blue, I yellow, I green. How many different ways can you fit any 3 of the rectangles into the outline of the rocket in .

Ribbon lengths

● **Use a ruler to measure a length in centimetres**

You need:
●● ruler

Estimate, then measure in centimetres the length of each prize ribbon.

Example

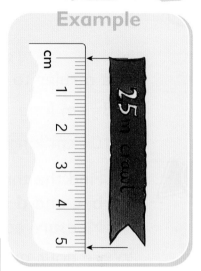

a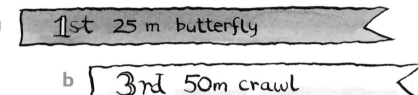
1st 25 m butterfly

b
3rd 50m crawl

c
2nd 25m back stroke

Estimate first, then measure the length of each prize ribbon to the nearest centimetre. Record your answers in a table.

Ribbon	Estimate	Measure
a	9 cm	
b		
c		

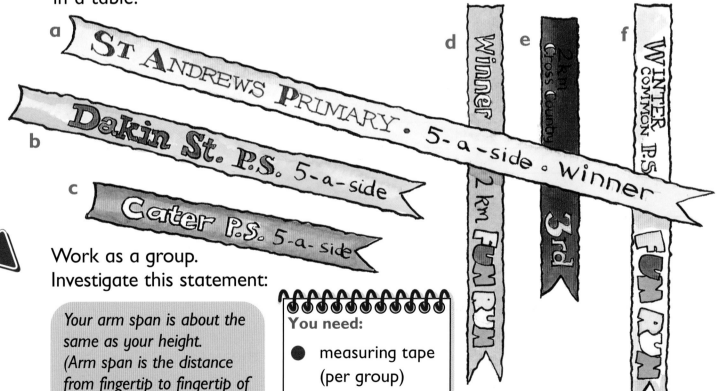

Work as a group.
Investigate this statement:

*Your arm span is about the same as your height.
(Arm span is the distance from fingertip to fingertip of outstretched arms.)*

You need:
● measuring tape (per group)

29

Web lengths

● **Use a ruler to measure to the nearest half centimetre**

You need:
● ruler

Example: $\leftarrow 2\frac{1}{2}$ cm $\rightarrow$

Use a ruler to draw lines which are

❶ Find the threads marked **a, b, c** and **d** in the web. Measure each thread.

Write your answers to the nearest $\frac{1}{2}$ cm.

❷ Now find the threads **e – i**. Copy and complete this table. Record your answers using decimal notation.

Thread	Estimate	Measure
e		
f		
g		
h		
i		

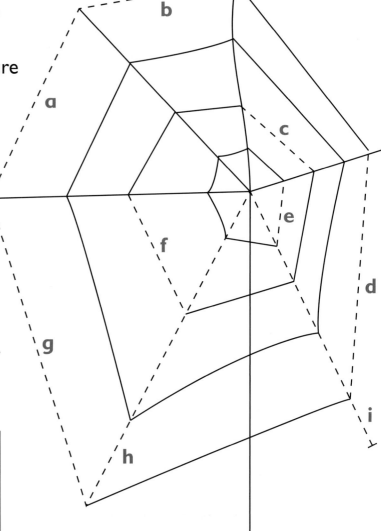

❶ The spider climbs halfway up the thread. How many centimetres has it still to climb to reach the centre of its web?

❷ A second spider builds a web which is double the size of the web above. How many centimetres long are each of the threads **a** to **i**?

Every silken thread in my web is a different length.

Whole or half metre measuring

● **Use a ruler or a tape measure to measure a length to the nearest half centimetre or half metre**

1 Estimate these distances to the nearest whole or half centimetre.

a A to B __4½ cm__

b A to C _____

c A to D _____

d A to E _____

e A to F _____

f A to G _____

G

C

B

A

F

D

E

2 Now measure each of the distances in question **1**. Write down your measurements.

Work with a partner.
Find six pairs of objects.
Estimate, then measure the distance between them.
Draw a table. Record your

Distance between	Estimate	Measure
2 tables	4 m	4½ m

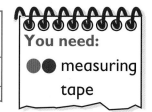

You need:

●● measuring tape

answers to the nearest whole or half metre. Here are some ideas for measuring.

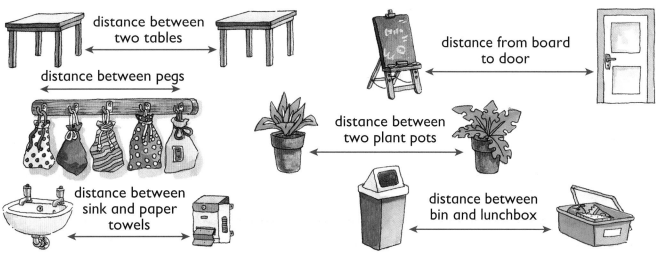

distance between two tables

distance from board to door

distance between pegs

distance between two plant pots

distance between sink and paper towels

distance between bin and lunchbox

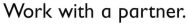

Work with a partner.
Estimate and measure each others,, height to the nearest whole cm.

Playground pictograms

 ❶ Copy the table. Count the children on each ride. Write the totals in the table.

Ride	Number of children
Swings	
Roundabout	
Slide	

❷ Copy the table. Count the children with different colours of shorts. Write the totals in the table.

Colour	Number of children
Red	
Blue	
Yellow	

Rides

Swings

Roundabout

Slide

Number of
children

Colour of shorts

Red

Blue

Yellow

Number of
children

1 Copy the pictograms.

2 Draw ☺ for each child in both pictograms.

3 Copy and complete the sentences.

There are ☐ children on the slide.

☐ children have red shorts.

You need:

●● squared paper

1 Count the flowers of each colour in the picture on page 32 and make a table.

Colour	Number of flowers

2 Copy and complete the pictogram.

Flower colours

Colour

Number of flowers

☐ stands
for 1 flower

33

Curtains bar chart

● **Show information using tables and bar charts**

 Count how many pairs of curtains there are of each colour. Copy and complete the table.

Colour	Number
Red	
Blue	
Yellow	
Green	
White	

Copy and complete the bar chart for the table on page 34.

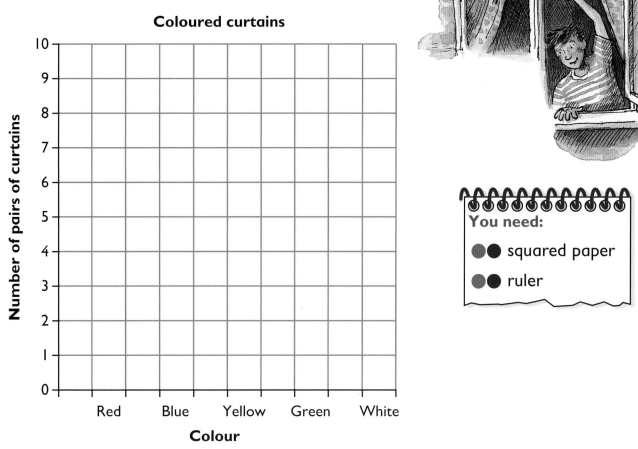

Coloured curtains

You need:
●● squared paper
●● ruler

1 Which colour is most common?

2 There are more blue pairs than red pairs of curtains. How many more?

3 How many pairs of curtains are not blue?

The table shows the colours of people's curtains in a different block.

Draw a bar chart to show the information.

Colour	Number of people
Blue	7
Yellow	4
White	9
Red	6
Other	10

Ice cream frequency

● **Explain what a frequency table says**

1 Copy the table. Count each kind of ice cream and complete the table.

Ice cream	Frequency
Ice lolly	
Ice cream cone	
Choc-ice	
Ice cream tub	

2 Use the information in the table to answer these questions.

   a How many ice cream tubs are there?

   b What is the frequency of ice lollies?

   c Which kind of ice cream is there most of?

   d Which kind of ice cream is there least of?

   e How many more ice cream cones are there than choc ices?

3 Write a sentence about the information displayed in your table.

toffee   strawberry   vanilla   chocolate   mint

1 Some children bought their favourite ice cream. Copy the table. Count the number of each flavour and complete the table.

Flavour	Frequency

2 Use the information in the table to answer these questions.

a How many chocolate ice creams are there?

b Which is the most popular flavour?

c How many children bought vanilla or toffee ice creams.

d How many more strawberry ice creams were bought than vanilla ice creams?

e Which flavour has a frequency of 5?

f How many children did not buy a strawberry ice cream?

Ask 24 children in your class which of the flavours in the ⬤ section is their favourite ice cream flavour. Make a frequency table and compare the results with the ⬤ table. Write a sentence about the information displayed in your table.

Party pictograms

● Show information using pictograms and bar charts

1 Copy this pictogram. Draw a circle ◯ for each balloon colour.
Write a key for your pictogram.

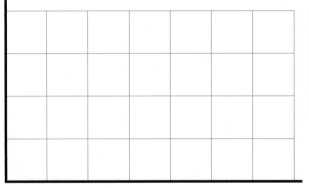

Balloon colours

red
blue
yellow
orange

Number of balloons

Key

2 Use the information in the completed pictogram to answer these questions.
  a How many balloons are red?
  b How many balloons are blue?
  c How many balloons are not yellow?
  d Which is the most common colour?
  e Which is the least common colour?
  f How many balloons are there altogether?

3 Write a sentence about the information displayed in your pictogram.

1 Copy this pictogram.
Decide on a simple picture to stand for two people.
On the chart draw that picture for every two people.
Write a key for your pictogram.

People at the party

police officers						
judges						
fire fighters						
sailors						

Key

Number of people

2 Use the information in the completed pictogram to answer these questions.
  a How many judges are at the party?
  b How many police officers are at the party?
  c Which is the most common kind of fancy dress?
  d How many more police officers than sailors are there?
  e How many people did not dress up as fire fighters?
  f How many people are at the party altogether?

3 Write a sentence about the information displayed in your pictogram.

 Draw a bar chart to show the number of people at the party in the ● section.

Space diagrams

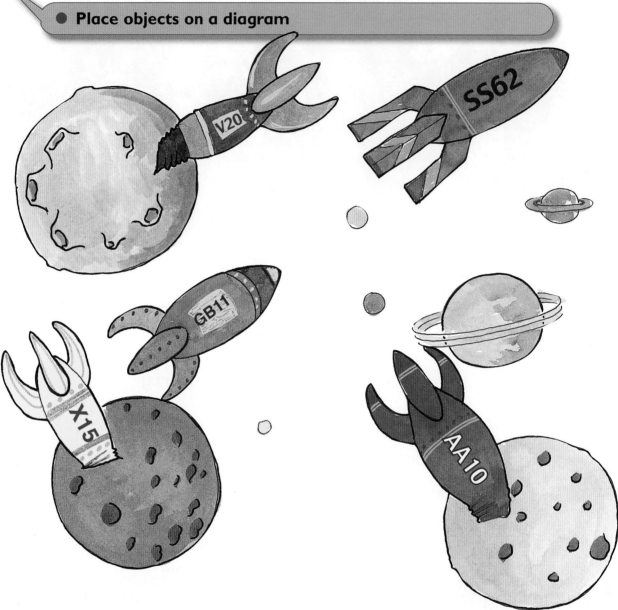

 Some of the rockets have crashed into planets.

1 Look at the rockets on both pages. Copy the diagram.

2 Write the rocket names on your diagram.

3 How many rockets have crashed?

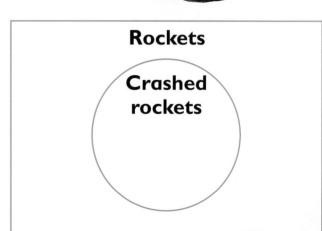

Rockets

Crashed rockets

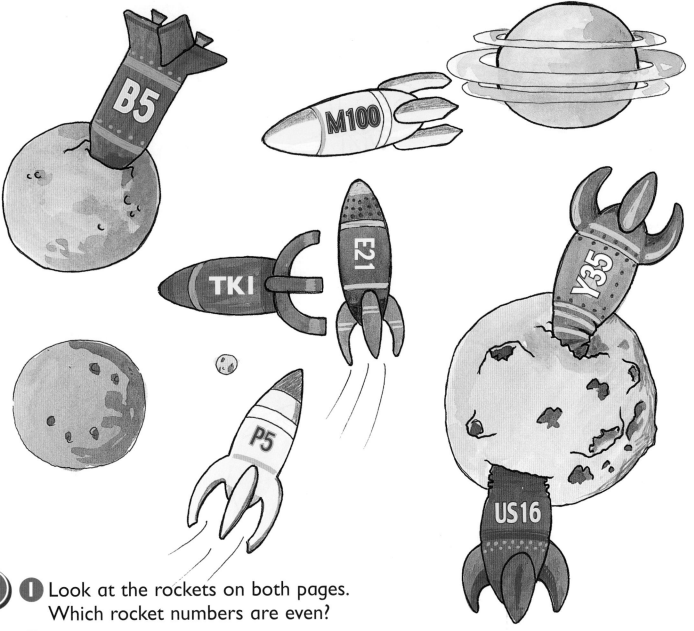

 1 Look at the rockets on both pages. Which rocket numbers are even?

2 Draw a diagram to show them.

3 How many rockets do not have even numbers?

Copy this diagram. Write the rocket names on your diagram. Draw a different diagram for odd and even rockets.

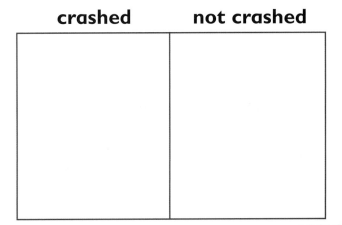

crashed	not crashed

Sweet Venn diagrams

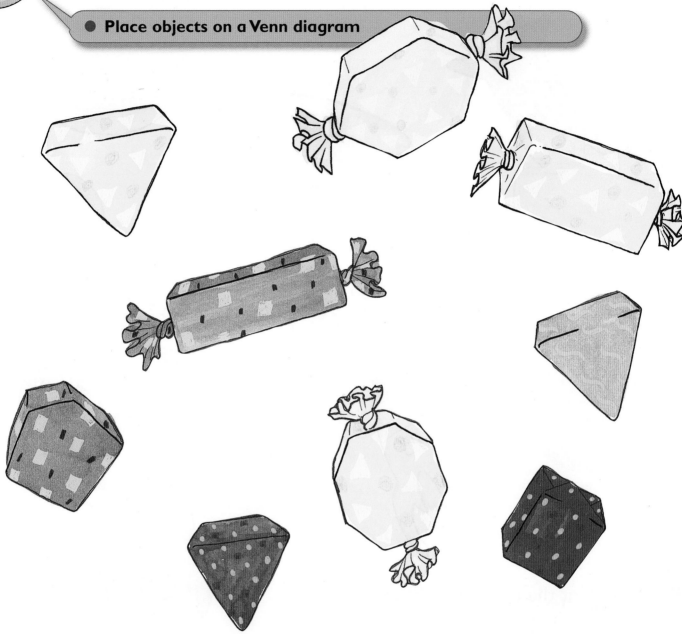

1. Look at the sweets on both pages. Copy the diagram.

2. Make a cross for each sweet.

3. How many sweets are red?

4. How many sweets are red or blue?

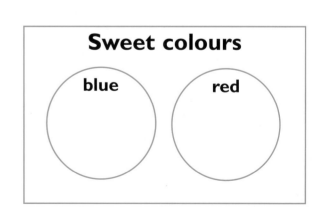

Sweet colours

blue   red

 ① Look at the sweets on both pages.
Copy the diagram.

② Make a cross for each sweet.

③ How many sweets are triangular?

④ How many sweets are not square shaped?

⑤ What do the crosses outside the circles
stand for?

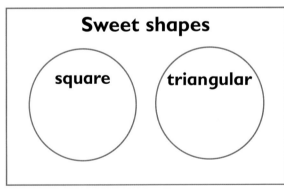

Sweet shapes

square   triangular

Make up your own Venn diagram for the sweets.

Windows

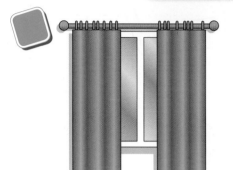   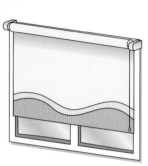

The table shows the window coverings of a row of houses.

Window covering	Frequency
Curtains	8
Horizontal blinds	5
Vertical blinds	2
Roller blinds	4
None	3

1 How many windows do not have any covering?

2 What is the most common window covering?

3 What does the frequency for vertical blinds tell you?

4 What is the total number of windows recorded?

5 Copy and complete the pictogram.

Front window coverings

Curtains

Horizontal blinds

Vertical blinds

Roller blinds

None

○ stands
for 1 window

Front window coverings

1 Copy and complete the bar chart to show the window coverings.

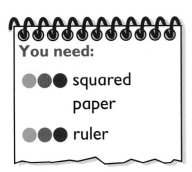

You need:
● ● ● squared paper
● ● ● ruler

Number of windows

Type of window covering

2 a Copy the diagram.

b Draw a tick for each window covering.

c How many windows do not have curtains or roller blinds?

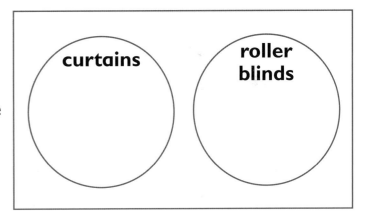

curtains

roller blinds

1 Ask 20 children for the type of coverings on their front windows.

2 Record the information in a frequency table.

3 Draw a pictogram to show your results.

4 Draw a bar chart to show your results.

5 Which is the most common type of window covering?

6 Compare your results with another person. Write a sentence.

45

Fruity addition

● **Add mentally one-digit and two-digit numbers**

Add the one-digit number by jumping to
the next ten. Show your working.

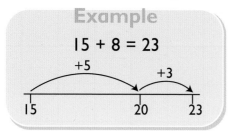

Example

15 + 8 = 23

+5   +3

15   20   23

Frank's fresh fruit

■
a 15 + 7   b 28 + 9   c 26 + 6
d 34 + 8   e 17 + 7   f 39 + 9
g 35 + 6   h 48 + 8   i 44 + 7
j 56 + 9   k 47 + 5   l 39 + 4

●
a 27 + 9   b 28 + 7   c 46 + 8
d 39 + 6   e 46 + 9   f 57 + 8
g 68 + 9   h 88 + 7   i 67 + 6
j 86 + 8   k 98 + 8   l 79 + 7
m 96 + 7   n 126 + 8   o 119 + 6
p 143 + 8   q 167 + 5   r 158 + 4

Make up your own calculations and use this strategy without drawing the
number line.

Fruity subtraction

● Subtract mentally one-digit and two-digit numbers

Subtract the one-digit number by jumping back
to the next ten. Show your working.

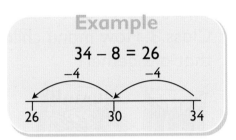

Example

$$34 - 8 = 26$$

a 24 – 6   b 25 – 8   c 22 – 5

d 32 – 6   e 36 – 9   f 31 – 7

g 42 – 5   h 45 – 8   i 44 – 6

j 52 – 3   k 54 – 5   l 57 – 9

a 25 – 8   b 32 – 7   c 37 – 9

d 44 – 8   e 47 – 9   f 52 – 7

g 55 – 8   h 68 – 9   i 63 – 6

j 74 – 6   k 83 – 5   l 94 – 8

m 97 – 9   n 106 – 7   o 104 – 9

p 116 – 8   q 128 – 9   r 135 – 7

Make up your own calculations and use this strategy without drawing the
empty number lines.

The problem classroom

● **Solve one-step and two-step problems involving numbers**

Solve these word problems. Show all your working.

a There are 19 girls and 7 boys in Class 3. How many children is that altogether?

b There are 24 pencils in the class. If 7 are lost, how many will be left?

c There are 28 children in the class. 9 children have finished their work for the display. How many children still need to finish theirs?

d Each of these 3 children have read 8 books this week. How many books have they read altogether?

a There are 56 colouring pencils. 8 are lost and 9 are broken. How many are left?

b There are 48 children in the hall and 8 more come in. The head teacher says that when the last 7 arrive they will all be here. How many children will there be altogether?

c There are 7 classes in the school. Every class sends 8 children to the library. How many children go to the library altogether?

d Check your answers to **a**, **b** and **c**.

Write a word problem for a friend to solve.

A piece of cake

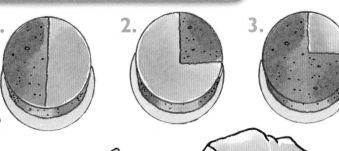

1 The baker is icing some cakes.

   a Which cake is half iced?

   b Which cake is a quarter iced?

   c Which cake is three quarters iced?

2 How many buns are on half of each tray?

a
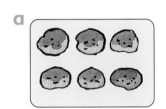

b

c
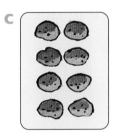

d
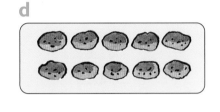

1 Using words, for each cake write down the fraction that has red icing.

a
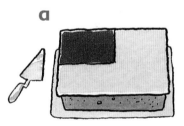

b
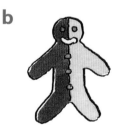

c
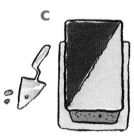

d

2 Using numbers, for each cake write down the fraction that has yellow icing.

3 How many buns in a quarter of each tray?

a
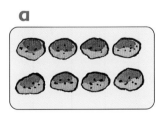

b
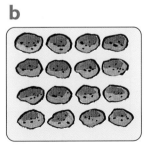

c
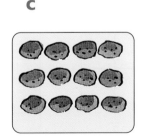

d
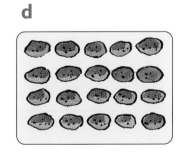

Explain what both numbers mean in the fractions $\frac{1}{2}$, $\frac{1}{3}$ and $\frac{1}{4}$.

Tiled fractions

● Recognise and find simple fractions of numbers or quantities

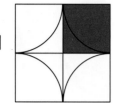 1   2    3 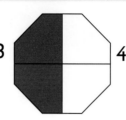   4    5    6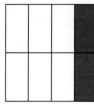

1 a Which tiles are half red?   **b** Which tiles are a quarter red?

   c Which tiles are a third red?

2 How many tiles are in one third of each pattern?

a   **b**   **c**    **d**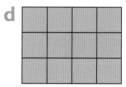

1 Write down the fraction of each tile that is blue.

a 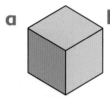   **b** 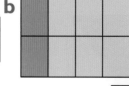   **c** 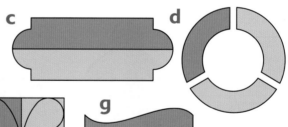   **d**

You need:
- squared paper
- colouring pencils

e   **f**   **g**

2 Draw these tiles on squared paper. Colour the tiles to match the fraction underneath.

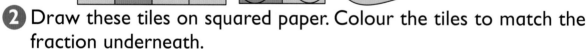

a $\frac{1}{2}$ **b** $\frac{1}{2}$ **c** $\frac{1}{4}$ **d** $\frac{1}{4}$ **e** $\frac{1}{3}$ **f** $\frac{1}{3}$

Explain how to work out how much of a shape is shaded.

Problematic lengths

● **Draw and measure lengths to the nearest half centimetre**

Draw lines of these lengths.

a $3\frac{1}{2}$ cm b $7\frac{1}{2}$ cm

c $10\frac{1}{2}$ cm d $14\frac{1}{2}$ cm

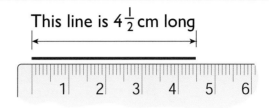

This line is $4\frac{1}{2}$ cm long

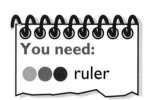

You need:
●●● ruler

This line is $5\frac{1}{2}$ cm + 5 cm = $10\frac{1}{2}$ cm long

5·5 cm   5 cm

1 Draw lines of these lengths.

a 7 cm longer than $4\frac{1}{2}$ cm

b $3\frac{1}{2}$ cm longer than 8 cm

c 6 cm shorter than $12\frac{1}{2}$ cm

d $7\frac{1}{2}$ cm shorter than 10 cm

e Twice as long as $3\frac{1}{2}$ cm

f Twice as long as $6\frac{1}{2}$ cm

g Half as long as 9 cm

h Half as long as 15 cm

2 Bendy straw A measures 10 cm   Bendy straw B measures 15 cm

A

$3\frac{1}{2}$ cm

$6\frac{1}{2}$ cm

$6\frac{1}{2}$ cm + $3\frac{1}{2}$ cm = 10 cm

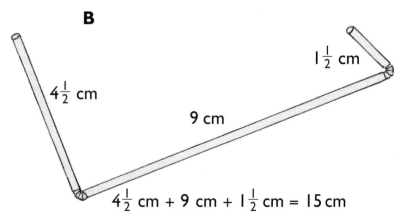

B

$1\frac{1}{2}$ cm

$4\frac{1}{2}$ cm

9 cm

$4\frac{1}{2}$ cm + 9 cm + $1\frac{1}{2}$ cm = 15 cm

a Draw 4 bendy straws like straw A. Make them bend in different places. Show your calculations below each drawing.

b Draw 4 bendy straws like straw B. Make them bend in different places. Show your calculations below each drawing.

Draw a 20 cm straw which bends in 3 places. Show your calculations below the drawing.

Card shop problems

● Solve word problems involving length

Find the correct envelope for each card.

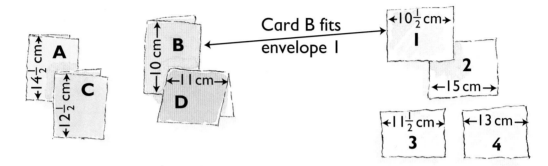

Card B fits envelope 1

Work out the answers to these word problems.

1 A birthday banner is 1 m 40 cm long.
What is the total length of 2 banners?

2 Two rolls of streamers are 45 cm and 54 cm long.

  a What is their total length?

  b What is the difference in their lengths?

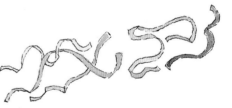

3 Pens are made in three sizes.
Small $8\frac{1}{2}$ cm, medium 12 cm, large $17\frac{1}{2}$ cm.
How much longer is the large pen than

  a the medium pen?

  b the small pen?

4 A roll of wrapping paper is $17\frac{1}{2}$ metres long.
Mary Ellen cuts off $3\frac{1}{2}$ metres to wrap a large gift.
What length of paper is left?

Ronnie said 'My pencil case is 25 cm long.
If I have another 7 pencil cases and place them
end to end, it will make 2 metres.'
Is he correct? Show how you worked out your answer.

Find your place

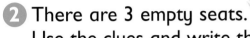

● Describe and find the position of a square on a grid of squares with rows and columns labelled

Look at the aircraft seating plan.

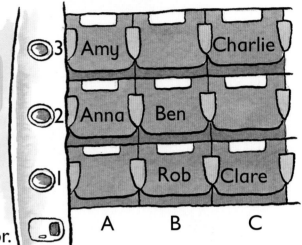

① Write the seat number for

   a Rob   b Amy

   c Charlie   d Anna

Example

Clare is in seat C1

② There are 3 empty seats.
   Use the clues and write the seat number for:

   a Liz who will sit between Amy and Charlie.

   b Owen who will sit next to Ben.

   c Sam who wants a seat nearest to the door.

Look at the hotel room plan.

① Name the guests in these rooms.

   a A1   b A4   c B3
   d C2   e D4   f C5

② Write the room number for these guests.

   a Lisa   e Jack
   b Jenny   f Andrew
   c Sophie   g Isabelle
   d Megan   h Tim

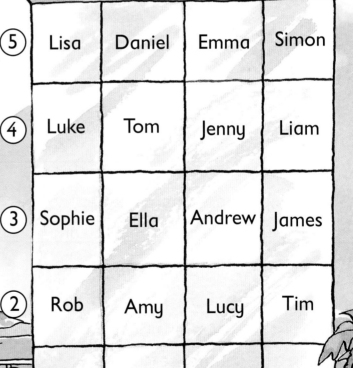

Tom and Simon swap rooms. Write their new room numbers.

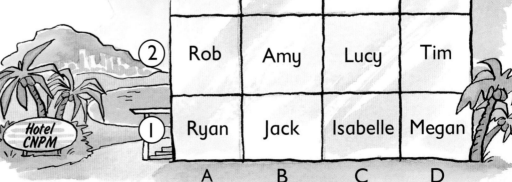

Keytag Island

- **Describe and find the position of a square on a grid of squares with rows and columns labelled**

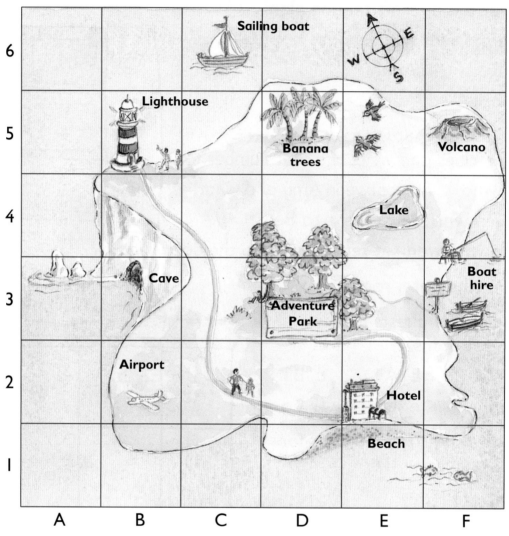

 Which square contains the:

a hotel   b airport   c volcano   d cave   e lighthouse

1 What will you find in:

a F3   b D5   c D3   d C6   e E1   f E4

2 List the squares you pass through on a trip from the hotel to:

a the lighthouse

b the cave

You hire a boat for the day. List the squares you pass through on a trip to the cave.

Time out

● **Read the time to 5 minutes on an analogue clock and a 12-hour digital clock**

 1 Copy and complete these five minute patterns.

a 3:00, 3:05, 3:10, ——, ——, ——, 3:30.

b 4:25, 4:30, 4:35, ——, ——, ——, ——.

c 8:45, 8:50, ——, ——, ——, ——.

2 Write the time these clocks show in digital form.

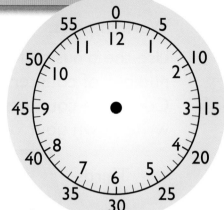

a    b    c    d

 1 Write these times in two ways.

a `2:30`   b `9:55`   c `1:35`

d `6:50`   e `12:45`   f `8:05`

Example

7:40

40 minutes past 7

20 minutes to 8

2 These children have check-up appointments with the school dentist.

Mark's appointment is at `3:45`

Write the appointment time for

a Emma, 10 minutes before Mark

b Neil, 10 minutes after Mark

c Omar, 20 minutes before Mark

d Rachel, 20 minutes after Mark.

 Write these appointment times in order, starting with the earliest.

10:00 a.m.   9:05 a.m.   4:25 p.m.   11:40 a.m.   1:50 p.m.   12:35 p.m.

Fabulous fractions

● **Find simple fractions of numbers**

 Work in pairs.

Use the trays to help you to divide the different number of counters into equal groups. Count the counters in one group and write down your answer.

Example

Divide 9 into thirds

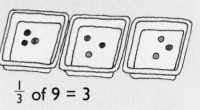

$\frac{1}{3}$ of 9 = 3

Thirds

Quarters

Fifths

You need:
● 20 counters
● sorting trays

a Divide 8 into quarters
b Divide 12 into thirds
c Divide 10 into fifths
d Divide 16 into quarters
e Divide 15 into fifths
f Divide 20 into fifths

HINT

$\frac{2}{3}$ of 9:
$\frac{1}{3}$ of 9 = 3
so $\frac{2}{3}$ of 9 is 3 + 3
which is 6.

① Find these fractions of numbers.
Look at the method used in the ▨ section to help you.

a $\frac{1}{3}$ of 15
b $\frac{1}{4}$ of 16
c $\frac{1}{5}$ of 15
d $\frac{1}{3}$ of 21

e $\frac{1}{4}$ of 20
f $\frac{1}{5}$ of 30
g $\frac{1}{3}$ of 30
h $\frac{1}{2}$ of 36

② Explain how to find a quarter of a number.

 ① a What does $\frac{2}{3}$ mean?
b What is $\frac{2}{3}$ of 12?

② a What does $\frac{3}{4}$ mean?
b What is $\frac{3}{4}$ of 12?

Fractions quiz

● **Find simple fractions of numbers and quantities**

Share the sweets evenly. How many sweets does each child get?

a   b   c   d   e   f

Answer the following problems. If you need to, use counters to help.

a What is half of 16? 	**b** Is this jar  $\frac{1}{10}$ full $\frac{1}{2}$ full or $\frac{3}{4}$ full?	**c** How many cakes does each person get? 	**d** What fraction of the slab has been eaten? 
e What fraction of the chocolates has been eaten? 	**f** Copy this grid. Colour $\frac{1}{10}$. 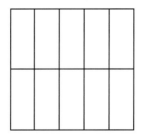	**g** How many cakes does each child get? 	**h** What fraction of sheep are in the pen? 

i What is $\frac{1}{3}$ of 15?

j In **c** and **g**, what fraction of the cakes does each child get?

What fraction of sweets have been opened?

a   b   c   d

Odds and evens

● **Identify patterns and relationships involving numbers, and use them to solve problems**

1 Jim says 'When you add two even numbers together the answer is always even.'

Is he right?

Choose different even numbers, add them together. Make up 10 different calculations. Are the answers they always even?

2 How many ways can you complete this calculation using two even numbers?

$$\boxed{} + \boxed{} = 18$$

1 Jamila says 'When you add an odd and an even number together the answer is sometimes odd and sometimes even.'

Do you think she is right?

How can you prove your answer?

2 How many ways can you complete this calculation using an odd and an even number?

$$\boxed{} + \boxed{} = 27$$

Investigate what happens when you add three odd numbers together. Explain why this is.

Calculation bricks

● **Know addition facts to 20**

Use the numbers on the bricks to build an addition calculation.

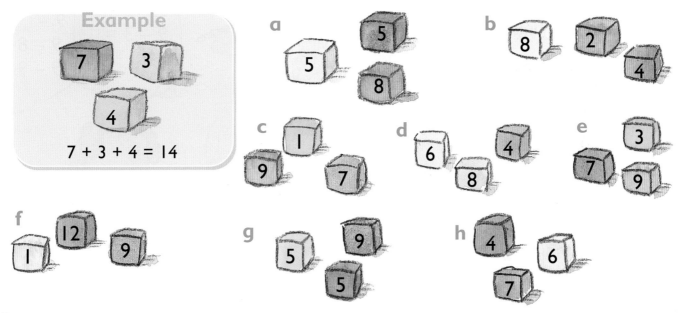

Example

7 + 3 + 4 = 14

a 5 5 8

b 8 2 4

c 1 9 7

d 6 4 8

e 3 7 9

f 12 1 9

g 5 9 5

h 4 6 7

① Use the numbers on the bricks to build an addition calculation.

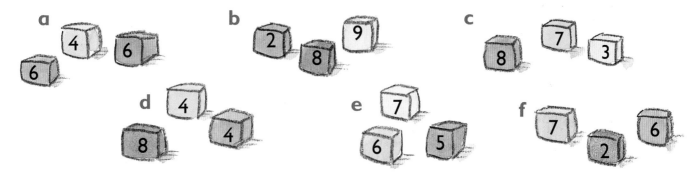

a 4 6 6

b 2 8 9

c 7 8 3

d 4 8 4

e 7 6 5

f 7 2 6

② Choose two calculations and explain why you added the numbers in that order.

① Use the numbers on the bricks to build an addition calculation.

a 6 15 2 3

b 5 7 19 2

c 12 3 6 9

② Choose one calculation and explain why you added the numbers in that order.

Subtraction facts book

● Know subtraction facts to 20

1 Steve has started working out the subtraction facts for 9.
Can you finish them?

9
9 − 0 = 9
9 − 1 = ☐
9 − 2 = ☐
9 − 3 = ☐
9 − ☐ = 5

9 − 5 = ☐
9 − ☐ = 3
9 − ☐ = 2
9 − 8 = ☐
9 − 9 = ☐

2 Helen has written some of the subtraction facts for 7.
Copy them out and write the remaining facts.

7 − 0 = 7
7 − 1 = 6
7 − 2 = 5
7 − 3 = 4

☐ − ☐ = ☐
☐ − ☐ = ☐
☐ − ☐ = ☐
☐ − ☐ = ☐

1 Jack has written the subtraction facts for 13.
Write out the calculations for 130 that these help him know the answers to.

13
13 − 0 = 13
13 − 1 = 12
13 − 2 = 11
13 − 3 = 10
13 − 4 = 9
13 − 5 = 8

13 − 6 = 7
13 − 7 = 6
13 − 8 = 5
13 − 9 = 4
13 − 10 = 3
13 − 11 = 2
13 − 12 = 1
13 − 13 = 0

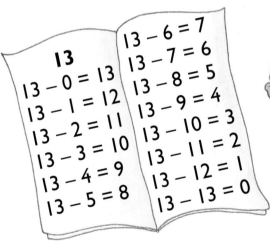

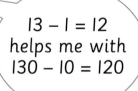

13 − 1 = 12
helps me with
130 − 10 = 120

2 Paul and Ella have chosen their numbers. Write the subtraction facts for them.

a  16

b  14

3 Pair Paul's facts with calculations starting with 160.

Find five different ways to jump back from 150 to 0, landing on multiples of ten.

0 ————————————————————— 150

Down by the billabong

● Describe the pattern when counting in 2s, 3s, 4s or 5s

Jack rabbit, the smallest animal, jumps in 2s, dingo jumps in 3s, wallaby jumps in 4s and kangaroo, who is the biggest, jumps in 5s.

On RCM: Down by the billabong, mark with a tick the stones to 40 that each animal will land on.

You need:

● Copy of RCM: Down by the billabong

1 Write the number of stones that each animal lands on.

2 Copy and complete the table.

Stones landed on	Number on stone
by 1 animal	2, 3
by 2 animals	4,
by 3 animals	
by 4 animals	

3 Write what you notice about the numbers on the stones on which 3 animals landed.

a Use the back of the RCM. Number the stones to 60 and head the columns for jumps in 2s, 3s, 4s and 5s.

b Complete each column with ticks at the appropriate stones.

c Write what you notice about the stone numbered 60.

Seats for all

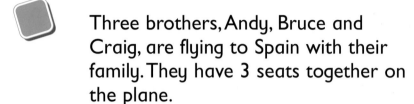

● **Make an organised list and look for patterns**

Three brothers, Andy, Bruce and Craig, are flying to Spain with their family. They have 3 seats together on the plane.

List all the possible ways they could take the three seats.

HINT

Make a list beginning with Andy.

Example

A	B	C
Andy in window seat	Bruce in middle seat	Craig in aisle seat

Last Saturday, Julie, Katy, Linda and May went to the cinema. They found four empty seats together in a row.

List all the possible ways they could sit together at the cinema.

Example

	Seat 1	Seat 2	Seat 3	Seat 4
1	J	K	L	M
2	J	K	M	L

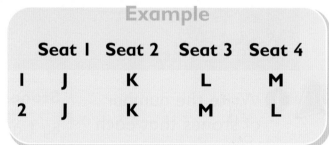

Remember

List the names in an ordered way and look for a pattern.

Next Saturday, Naomi is joining her four friends, Julie, Katy, Linda and May, on a visit to the cinema.

She still has her leg in plaster after a fall and has to sit in the first seat in the row. Find how many possible seating arrangements the five girls could have.

Time to multiply

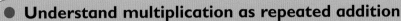

- **Understand multiplication as repeated addition**
- **Understand that multiplication can be done in any order**

1 Draw a picture to match these addition facts.
Write the total for each.

a 4 + 4 = ☐

b 3 + 3 + 3 + 3 = ☐

c 5 + 5 + 5 = ☐

d 2 + 2 + 2 + 2 + 2 = ☐

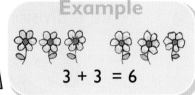

Example
3 + 3 = 6

2 Draw a picture to match these multiplication facts.
Write the total for each.

a 2 × 4 = ☐

b 4 × 3 = ☐

c 3 × 5 = ☐

d 5 × 2 = ☐

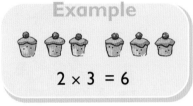

Example
2 × 3 = 6

3 Look carefully at your pictures. What do you notice?

1 Write an addition and a multiplication number sentence for each set of dice.

a

3 + 3 + 3 + 3 = ☐
4 × 3 = ☐

b

c

d

e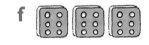

f

2 Write two multiplication facts for each set of pictures.

a

b

c

d

Write a division fact for each set of pictures in question **2** of the ⬤ section.

Divide by...?

- Understand division as grouping or sharing
- Recognise that division is the inverse of multiplication

 Write a division fact for each set of pictures.

a

Example

$20 \div 2 = 10$

b  c

d   e

 Write two multiplication and two division facts for each set of pictures.

Example
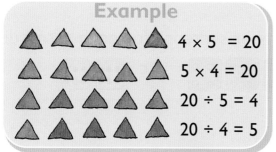
$4 \times 5 = 20$
$5 \times 4 = 20$
$20 \div 5 = 4$
$20 \div 4 = 5$

a  b

c  d  e

 Write two multiplication and two division facts for both sets of numbers.

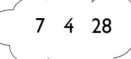 7 4 28

 5 9 45

3 times table

$2 \times 3 = 6$

● **Begin to know the 3 times table**

1 Jamil went in search of the giant's castle. He jumped along the stepping stones and made jumps of three each time.
Copy Jamil's table and write down all the numbers he jumped on.

$10 \times 3 = 30$

Number of jumps	1	2	3	4	5	6	7	8	9	10
Landing number	3	6								

Example
$1 \times 3 = 3$
$2 \times 3 =$

2 Write out the 3 times table.

$5 \times 3 = 15$

The answers to the 3 times table are locked away in the treasure chest. Search this page for the key facts and use them to help you find the answers.

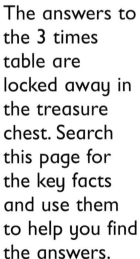

a $2 \times 3 =$
   $5 \times 3 =$
   $10 \times 3 =$
   $1 \times 3 =$

b $4 \times 3 =$
   $7 \times 3 =$
   $3 \times 3 =$
   $9 \times 3 =$

c $6 \times 3 =$
   $0 \times 3 =$
   $8 \times 3 =$
   $11 \times 3 =$

d $\bigcirc \times 3 = 15$
   $\bigcirc \times 3 = 30$
   $\bigcirc \times 3 = 9$
   $\bigcirc \times 3 = 3$

e $3 \times \bigcirc = 12$
   $3 \times \bigcirc = 27$
   $\bigcirc \times 3 = 24$
   $\bigcirc \times 3 = 6$

f $3 \times \bigcirc = 21$
   $3 \times \bigcirc = 18$
   $\bigcirc \times 3 = 9$
   $\bigcirc \times \bigcirc = 33$

Write down the answers to each pair of calculations. What do you notice?

$2 \times 3 =$
$2 \times 6 =$

$4 \times 3 =$
$4 \times 6 =$

$5 \times 3 =$
$5 \times 6 =$

$7 \times 3 =$
$7 \times 6 =$

$1 \times 3 = 3$

3's a problem!

- Begin to know the 3 times table
- Solve word problems including numbers in 'real life' and money

Work out the answers to these problems. Show all your working.

 5p
 2p
 3p
 9p

a Buy 3 How much will you spend?

b A Chocobar costs 9p. How much will 3 cost?

c How much will 10 cost?

d Buy 3 What do you spend?

e 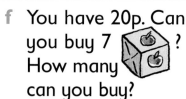 costs 3p How much will 4 cost?

f You have 20p. Can you buy 7 ? How many can you buy?

a Sarah made a clover headband by joining 8 clover stems together. How many leaves altogether?

b The tennis club bought 5 new packets of tennis balls. How many new tennis balls do they have?

c Flowers cost £4 a bunch. Lee spent £12. How many bunches did she buy?

d Imran needs 2 sets of wickets to play a game of cricket. How many stumps does he need?

e There are 3 cakes on each plate. There are 30 cakes altogether. How many plates are there?

f How many wheels altogether on 6 tricycles?

 Write your own word problem for each of these facts.

a $7 \times 3 =$ **b** $3 \times 4 =$ **c** $6 \div 3 =$ **d** $5 \times 3 =$

4 times table

● **Begin to know the 4 times table**

1 Build your own 4 times table.
Draw blocks of 4 to see the 4 times table grow.
Draw up to 10 × 4.

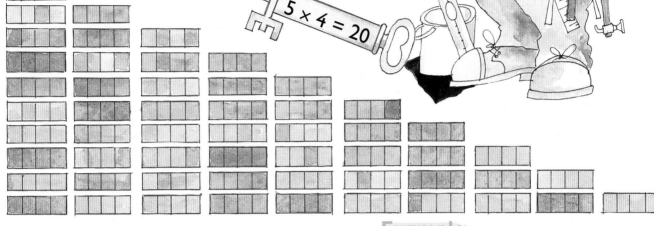

5 × 4 = 20

2 Write a multiplication fact for each block.

Example

1 × 4 = 4

10 × 4 = 40

1 The answers to the 4 times table are
locked away in the 'Secret Diary'.
Search this page for the key facts and use them to help you find the answers.

a		b		c	
5 × 4 = ☐		4 × 4 = ☐		3 × 4 = ☐	
2 × 4 = ☐		7 × 4 = ☐		9 × 4 = ☐	
10 × 4 = ☐		6 × 4 = ☐		8 × 4 = ☐	
1 × 4 = ☐		0 × 4 = ☐		11 × 4 = ☐	

Secret Diary
÷ 4

2 Write two multiplication facts for the dots in each picture.

a

b

c

Write two division facts for the dots in each picture in question **2** of the
● section.

1 × 4 = 4

2 × 4 = 8

The £4 sale

- Begin to know the 4 times table
- Solve word problems including numbers in money

Work out the answers to these word problems. Show all your working.

SALE
EVERYTHING
£4!

a Buy 6

How much do you spend?

b Buy 3

What is the total cost?

c Buy 5

How much are they altogether?

d Buy 10

How much money do you need?

e  cost £4

You buy 4. How much do you spend?

f cost £4

You buy 2. How much do you spend?

a There are 4 children in the Smith family. They each choose one toy. How much money is spent?

b Samina has a teddy bear collection. She spends £36 on teddies which cost £4 each. How many teddies does she buy?

c Jim bought 8 computer games each costing £4. What is the total cost?

d A school needs new books for the library. They buy 7 books. How much do they spend?

e Ivan has £40 to spend on toys. How many can he buy?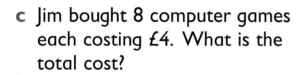

f Ahmed buys 2 board games. His sister Shelina buys 3 toy cars and a doll. How much do they spend altogether?

 Write your own word problems for each of these facts.

a 6×4 b $28 \div 4$ c 8×4 d $40 \div 4$

Doubling machines

● **Double numbers to at least 20**

Double the buttons on each machine. Write an addition and multiplication fact for each one.

a   b   c

d   e   f

g   h   i

Example

$$3 + 3 = 6$$
$$2 \times 3 = 6$$

① Write a multiplication fact for each number on these machines.

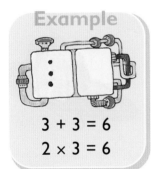
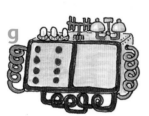

a 5 7 10 × 2 ☐ ☐ ☐

b 11 4 15 × 2 ☐ ☐ ☐

c 6 16 13 × 2 ☐ ☐ ☐

② Write an addition fact for each number on these machines.

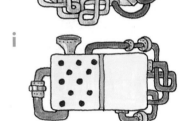
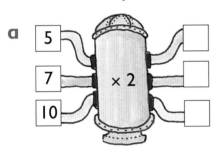
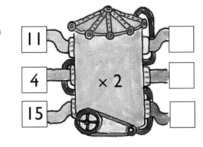
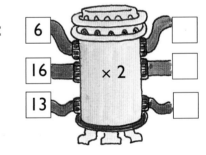
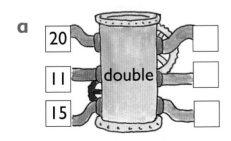
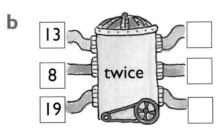
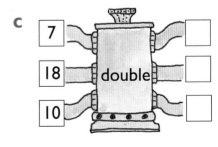

a 20 11 15 double ☐ ☐ ☐

b 13 8 19 twice ☐ ☐ ☐

c 7 18 10 double ☐ ☐ ☐

Write down 10 numbers between 20 and 50 and double each number.

Multiplying a 'teens' number

● **Multiply a 'teens' number by a one-digit number**

  1 Copy and complete.

a 10 × 4 =   b 10 × 8 =   c 10 × 2 =   d 10 × 9 =

e 10 × 3 =   f 10 × 1 =   g 10 × 5 =   h 10 × 6 =

2 Copy and complete.

a 9 × 3 =   b 7 × 4 =

c 8 × 3 =   d 6 × 4 =

e 9 × 2 =   f 3 × 5 =

g 7 × 5 =   h 6 × 3 =

Example

$16 × 4 = (10 × 4) + (6 × 4)$
$= 40 + 24$
$= 64$

Copy and complete.

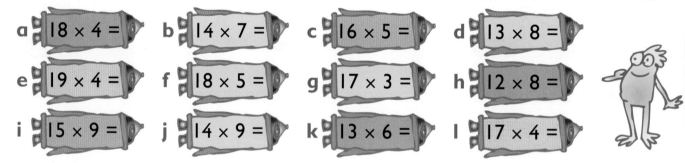

a 18 × 4 =   b 14 × 7 =   c 16 × 5 =   d 13 × 8 =

e 19 × 4 =   f 18 × 5 =   g 17 × 3 =   h 12 × 8 =

i 15 × 9 =   j 14 × 9 =   k 13 × 6 =   l 17 × 4 =

- Write down the number 1 and any two other digits, e.g. 1, 6 and 8.
- Make a 'teens' number and a one-digit number e.g. 16 and 8.
- Multiply the two numbers together.
- By re-arranging the three digits, investigate what other products you can make by multiplying a 'teens' number and a one-digit number.
- What is the largest answer you can make?
- What is the smallest answer you can make?

Maths Facts

Problem solving

The seven steps to problem solving

1. Read the problem carefully.
2. What do you have to find?
3. What facts are given?
4. Which of the facts do you need?
5. Make a plan.
6. Carry out your plan to obtain your answer.
7. Check your answer.

Number

Positive and negative numbers

Place value

1000	2000	3000	4000	5000	6000	7000	8000	9000
100	200	300	400	500	600	700	800	900
10	20	30	40	50	60	70	80	90
1	2	3	4	5	6	7	8	9

Number facts

Multiplication and division facts

	×1	×2	×3	×4	×5	×6	×7	×8	×9	×10
×1	1	2	3	4	5	6	7	8	9	10
×2	2	4	6	8	10	12	14	16	18	20
×3	3	6	9	12	15	18	21	24	27	30
×4	4	8	12	16	20	24	28	32	36	40
×5	5	10	15	20	25	30	35	40	45	50
×6	6	12	18	24	30	36	42	48	54	60
×7	7	14	21	28	35	42	49	56	63	70
×8	8	16	24	32	40	48	56	64	72	80
×9	9	18	27	36	45	54	63	72	81	90
×10	10	20	30	40	50	60	70	80	90	100

Fractions and decimals

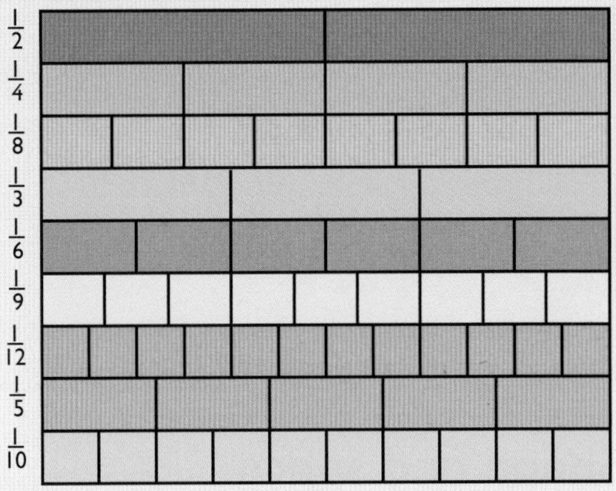

Calculations

Addition

Whole numbers

Example: 845 + 758

```
   845              845
 + 758     →      + 758
 -----            -----
  1500             1603
    90              1 1
    13
 -----
  1603
    1
```

Money

Example: £26.48 + £53.75

```
   £26.48              £26.48
 + £53.75     →      + £53.75
 --------            --------
    70.00              £80.23
     9.00               1 1 1
     1.10
     0.13
 --------
   £80.23
   1
```

Calculations

Subtraction

Example: 162 – 115

```
  162
 –  5
  157
 – 10
  147
 –100
   47
```

➡

```
  162
 –115
    5  → 120
   42  → 162
   47
```

➡

```
         50   12
  100 + 60 + 2
 –100 + 10 + 5
         40 + 7
```

➡

```
      5 12
    1 6 2
   – 115
      47
```

Multiplication

Example: 82 × 7

Grid method   or   Partitioning

82 × 7 = (80 × 7) + (2 × 7)
= 560 + 14
= 574

```
 ×    80    2
 7   560   14   = 574
```

```
    82
  ×  7
   560  (80 × 7)
    14  ( 2 × 7)
   574
```

➡

```
    82
  ×  7
   560
    14
   574
```

➡

```
    82
  ×  7
   574
     1
```

Division

Example: 87 ÷ 5

87 ÷ 5 = (50 + 37) ÷ 5
= (50 ÷ 5) + (37 ÷ 5)
= 10 + 7 R 2
= 17 R 2

or

```
     87
   – 50   (10 × 5)
     37
   – 35   ( 7 × 5)
      2
```
Answer   17 R 2

or

```
 5) 87
   – 50   (10 × 5)
     37
   – 35   ( 7 × 5)
      2
```
Answer   17 R 2

Shape and space

2–D shapes

circle | right-angled triangle | equilateral triangle | isosceles triangle | square | rectangle | pentagon | hexagon | heptagon | octagon

3–D shapes

cube | cuboid | cone | cylinder | sphere | triangular prism | triangular-based pyramid (tetrahedron) | square-based pyramid